The Meaning of Marriage

THE WORKBOOK

Copyright © 2023 by GuideGuru Publishing

All rights reserved. No part of this publication may be reproduced, distributed, or transmitted in any form or by any means, including photocopying, recording, or other electronic or mechanical methods, without the prior written permission of the publisher, except in the case of brief quotations embodied in critical reviews and certain other noncommercial uses permitted by copyright law. For permission requests, write to the publisher at the address below.

Disclaimer:

The content in this workbook is for informational purposes only and not a substitute for professional advice. Individual experiences may vary, and personal beliefs and cultural factors should be considered. Approach exercises with caution and discontinue if they cause distress. The author and publisher strive for accuracy but do not guarantee completeness or assume liability. External references are for convenience only. By using this workbook, you acknowledge that the author, publisher, and associated parties are not liable for any damages. Use your judgment and seek professional advice when needed.

Thank you for choosing to engage with this book. We hope it helps you build a healthy and loving relationship with your partner.

LESSONS IN THIS WORKBOOK:

1. The Secret of Marriage

2. The Power for Marriage

3. The Essence of Marriage

4. The Mission of Marriage

5. Loving the Stranger

6. Embracing the Other

Chapter 1: The Secret of Marriage

Lesson 1:

The Covenant of Marriage: Marriage is a sacred covenant between two individuals, built on love, commitment, and selflessness.

Reflect on your understanding of marriage as a covenant. Write a personal definition of what a covenant means to you and how it applies to marriage. Consider the responsibilities, commitments, and expectations that come with a covenantal relationship.

Write a letter to your partner or future partner, expressing your commitment to the covenant of marriage. Describe the qualities and actions that you believe are important in upholding this covenant. Share your intentions for fostering love, commitment, and selflessness in your relationship.

Think about a challenging situation or conflict you have faced in a past or current relationship. Reflect on how viewing the relationship as a covenant could have influenced your actions and choices. Write down specific steps you can take to approach future challenges with a covenantal mindset.

Lesson 2:

The Purpose of Marriage: Marriage is designed to bring about personal transformation and growth, as well as to reflect the love and grace of God.

Reflect on how marriage has impacted your personal growth and transformation. Write a journal entry describing specific ways in which your relationship has challenged and shaped you. Explore the lessons you have learned and the qualities you have developed through your marital journey.

Write a reflection on how your marriage can be a reflection of God's love and grace. Describe the ways in which you can embody love, forgiveness, and compassion in your relationship. Discuss how your actions and attitudes can serve as a testimony of God's presence in your marriage.

Imagine yourself at the end of a long and fulfilling life with your partner. Write a letter to your future self, describing the growth and transformation you hope to experience in your marriage. Reflect on the legacy you want to leave through your relationship and the impact you want to have on your partner and those around you.

Lesson 3:

The Mystery of Marriage: Marriage is a profound mystery that mirrors the relationship between Christ and the Church, revealing the depth and beauty of God's love.

Write a personal reflection on the mystery of marriage. Describe the ways in which your marriage has revealed glimpses of God's love and grace. Reflect on moments of connection, forgiveness, or sacrifice that have deepened your understanding of the divine mystery within your relationship.

Reflect on the qualities of Christ's love for the Church, such as sacrificial love, forgiveness, and unconditional acceptance. Write down specific actions you can take to embody these qualities in your marriage. Consider how you can create an atmosphere of love and grace that reflects the mystery of Christ's love.

Write a prayer for your marriage, expressing gratitude for the mystery and beauty it holds. Pray for guidance, wisdom, and strength to continually deepen your understanding and experience of God's love through your relationship. Reflect on how you can incorporate this prayer into your regular spiritual practices.

Chapter 2: The Power for Marriage

Lesson 1:

God's Design for Marriage: Marriage is intended to be a lifelong commitment, grounded in God's design for human relationships and the union of two distinct individuals.

Reflect on your understanding of God's design for marriage. Write a journal entry describing the qualities and values that you believe God intends for marriages to embody. Consider the roles, responsibilities, and mutual respect that are essential in honoring this design.

Write a letter to your partner or future partner, expressing your commitment to align your marriage with God's design. Discuss specific actions and behaviors you can implement to nurture and honor this sacred commitment. Share your aspirations for building a strong foundation based on God's principles.

Think about a challenging situation or conflict you have faced in your marriage or previous relationships. Reflect on how viewing your relationship through the lens of God's design could have influenced your responses and decisions. Write down specific steps you can take to align your actions with God's intended design for your marriage.

___
___
___
___
___
___
___
___
___
___
___
___
___
___
___
___
___
___
___
___
___
___
___
___
___
___
___
___
___
___
___

Lesson 2:

The Role of Love and Grace: Love and grace are essential in sustaining a marriage. Cultivating a selfless love and extending grace towards one another can overcome challenges and build a strong foundation.

Reflect on your understanding of selfless love within marriage. Write a personal definition of what selfless love means to you and how it manifests in a marital relationship. Consider the actions, attitudes, and sacrifices that are involved in cultivating selfless love.

Write a reflection on the role of grace in your marriage. Describe specific instances where you have experienced or witnessed grace from your partner or extended grace yourself. Reflect on the impact that extending and receiving grace has had on your relationship.

Think about a recent disagreement or conflict in your marriage. Write a letter to your partner, expressing love and grace in the midst of that situation. Describe the ways in which you can extend grace, understanding, and forgiveness, and share your commitment to working through challenges with love and selflessness.

Lesson 3:

The Influence of Faith: Faith in God provides the strength, wisdom, and guidance necessary to navigate the complexities of marriage and fulfill its purpose.

Reflect on the role of faith in your own life and its influence on your marriage. Write a journal entry describing the ways in which your faith has provided strength, wisdom, and guidance in navigating the challenges of marriage.

Write a prayer for your marriage, expressing gratitude for the influence of faith in your relationship. Pray for God's guidance, wisdom, and grace to be present in your marriage. Reflect on how you can incorporate this prayer into your regular spiritual practices.

Write a letter to yourself, reminding you of the importance of faith in your marriage. Discuss specific actions you can take to nurture your faith and deepen your spiritual connection with your partner. Consider how you can incorporate spiritual practices, such as prayer, meditation, or attending religious services, to strengthen your bond and seek guidance together.

Chapter 3: The Essence of Marriage

Lesson 1:

Companionship and Friendship: Marriage is a deep bond of companionship and friendship, characterized by shared interests, emotional support, and mutual respect.

Write a list of shared interests and activities that you and your partner enjoy or would like to explore together. Reflect on the importance of these shared experiences in fostering companionship and friendship. Make a commitment to regularly engage in these activities to strengthen your bond.

Reflect on a specific moment when your partner provided emotional support during a challenging time. Write a letter of gratitude to your partner, expressing appreciation for their role as a companion and friend. Describe the impact of their support on your well-being and the strength of your relationship.

Create a vision board or collage that represents the companionship and friendship you aspire to have in your marriage. Include images, quotes, and symbols that symbolize shared interests, emotional connection, and mutual respect. Display this visual representation in a prominent place as a reminder of your commitment to nurturing companionship and friendship in your marriage.

Lesson 2:

Intimacy and Selflessness: True intimacy in marriage is cultivated through selflessness, vulnerability, and the willingness to prioritize the needs and well-being of one's spouse.

Reflect on a time when you felt truly seen and understood by your partner. Write a journal entry describing the elements of that experience that fostered intimacy. Consider the role of selflessness, vulnerability, and active listening in creating a safe space for emotional connection.

Write a letter to your partner, expressing your commitment to prioritizing their needs and well-being in your marriage. Discuss specific actions you can take to demonstrate selflessness and nurture intimacy. Share your intentions to create an environment of trust and vulnerability where both partners can freely express their emotions and needs.

Reflect on a recent conflict or disagreement in your marriage. Write a journal entry exploring how selflessness and vulnerability could have influenced the outcome of that situation. Consider alternative approaches that prioritize the well-being of your partner and promote a deeper understanding and connection.

Lesson 3:

The Pursuit of Oneness: Marriage is a journey of becoming one, where the differences and conflicts are navigated with understanding, compromise, and a shared commitment to unity.

Write a personal reflection on the concept of oneness in marriage. Describe what it means to you and how you envision achieving it with your partner. Reflect on the importance of understanding, compromise, and unity in navigating differences and conflicts.

Reflect on a recent disagreement or conflict in your marriage. Write a letter to your partner, expressing your commitment to unity and understanding. Share your thoughts on how you can work together to find common ground, foster compromise, and maintain a sense of unity amidst differences.

Create a list of three potential areas of conflict or difference that you anticipate may arise in your marriage. Write down strategies or approaches that can promote understanding, compromise, and unity in each of these areas. Make a commitment to proactively address these potential conflicts with a shared commitment to oneness and unity in mind.

Chapter 4:
The Mission of Marriage

Lesson 1:

Marriage and Vocation: Marriage is not only a personal relationship but also a shared vocation. It involves a joint mission to serve God, contribute to society, and fulfill the unique purposes and gifts of each partner.

Reflect on your individual gifts, talents, and passions. Write a personal mission statement that incorporates how you can use these qualities to serve God and contribute to society through your marriage. Consider how your partner's gifts align with yours and how you can support and complement each other in fulfilling your joint mission.

Write a letter to your partner, expressing your commitment to the shared vocation of marriage. Discuss specific actions and goals you can set together to live out your mission and serve God as a couple. Share your aspirations for making a positive impact in your community or the world.

Reflect on a specific instance where you and your partner worked together to serve others or fulfill a shared mission. Write a journal entry describing the experience, the impact it had, and the lessons you learned. Consider how you can continue to seek opportunities for joint service and mission in your marriage.

Lesson 2:

Parenting and Legacy: Parenthood is an important aspect of marriage, as couples have the opportunity to nurture and raise the next generation, passing on values, faith, and a legacy of love.

Reflect on your aspirations and values as parents. Write a letter to your future or current child, expressing your hopes, dreams, and intentions for their upbringing. Consider the legacy of love and values you want to pass on to them through your marriage.

Write a journal entry reflecting on your own upbringing and the positive aspects you would like to emulate in your own parenting. Identify specific actions or behaviors that reflect these values and commit to integrating them into your parenting approach.

Write a list of qualities and values that you want to instill in your children through your marriage. Consider how your own marriage can serve as a model for healthy relationships and love. Reflect on specific ways you can nurture these qualities and values in your parenting journey.

Lesson 3:

Marriage as Witness: A healthy and loving marriage can serve as a powerful witness to the world, reflecting God's design for relationships and inspiring others to pursue meaningful and committed partnerships.

Write a reflection on the impact your own marriage can have on others. Describe specific instances where you have seen your relationship serve as a witness to others. Reflect on the qualities, actions, or attitudes that have inspired and influenced those around you.

Write a letter to a younger couple or someone seeking advice on relationships, sharing insights and wisdom from your own marriage. Discuss the aspects of your relationship that you believe reflect God's design and offer guidance for building a healthy and loving partnership.

Reflect on the challenges or obstacles you have faced in your marriage and how you have overcome them. Write a journal entry describing the lessons you have learned and the growth you have experienced as a result. Consider how sharing these experiences can serve as a witness to others, offering hope and encouragement in their own marital journey.

Chapter 5: Loving the Stranger

Lesson 1:

Embracing Differences: Marriage involves navigating the challenges of loving someone who is different from oneself. Accepting and appreciating these differences can enrich the relationship and foster growth.

Reflect on a specific difference between you and your partner that has caused challenges or conflicts in your relationship. Write a journal entry exploring your feelings, thoughts, and beliefs about this difference. Practice empathy by putting yourself in your partner's shoes and considering their perspective. Identify ways in which you can appreciate and celebrate these differences to strengthen your relationship.

Write a letter to your partner expressing gratitude for the ways in which their differences have enriched your life and the relationship. Describe specific qualities or perspectives they bring that you admire or appreciate. Share your commitment to embracing and learning from these differences to foster growth and understanding.

Create a "Differences List" together with your partner. Write down a list of your unique qualities, interests, and preferences. Reflect on how these differences can complement and enhance your relationship. Use this list as a reminder to appreciate and value each other's individuality.

Lesson 2:

Conflict Resolution: Healthy conflict resolution is crucial in a marriage. It requires effective communication, active listening, empathy, and a commitment to finding mutually satisfying solutions.

Reflect on a recent conflict or disagreement you had with your partner. Write a journal entry describing the specific communication breakdowns or patterns that contributed to the conflict. Explore your role in the conflict and identify areas for improvement in your communication and conflict resolution skills.

Write a letter to your partner, expressing your commitment to healthy conflict resolution in your marriage. Share your intentions to actively listen, validate their feelings, and seek mutually satisfying solutions. Discuss specific strategies you can employ, such as using "I" statements, taking breaks when needed, and practicing empathy.

Think about a past conflict or disagreement that you successfully resolved as a couple. Write a reflection piece describing the communication strategies and skills you used to reach a resolution. Reflect on what you learned from that experience and how you can apply those lessons to future conflicts.

Lesson 3:

Forgiveness and Grace: Forgiveness and extending grace are essential in maintaining a healthy and thriving marriage. Choosing to forgive, heal, and move forward strengthens the bond and promotes emotional well-being.

Reflect on a past hurt or offense that you have forgiven in your marriage. Write a journal entry describing the process of forgiveness, including the emotions you experienced and the impact it had on your relationship. Reflect on the growth and healing that occurred as a result of extending grace.

Write a letter to yourself, exploring any lingering grudges or unresolved hurts in your marriage. Reflect on the importance of forgiveness and grace in moving forward. Challenge yourself to let go of any resentments and make a commitment to extend grace to your partner.

Create a forgiveness ritual with your partner. Write down specific steps or actions you can take together to cultivate forgiveness and healing in your marriage. This can include having open and honest conversations, seeking professional help if needed, or engaging in acts of love and kindness towards each other to rebuild trust and promote emotional well-being.

Chapter 6: Embracing the Other

Lesson 1:

Sacrificial Love: Marriage requires sacrificial love, characterized by putting the needs and desires of one's spouse above one's own. Selflessness is foundational in building a strong and lasting marital relationship.

Reflect on a recent situation where you had to choose between your own needs and desires and those of your partner. Write a journal entry describing the decision-making process and the outcome. Reflect on how your act of sacrificial love impacted your relationship and how you felt about the experience.

Write a letter to your partner, expressing your commitment to sacrificial love in your marriage. Discuss specific ways you can prioritize their needs and desires above your own. Share your intentions to foster a selfless attitude and explore the impact it can have on the strength and longevity of your relationship.

Think about a specific area in your relationship where you struggle to prioritize your partner's needs. Write down practical steps you can take to cultivate a more selfless approach in that area. Make a commitment to consistently practice sacrificial love in that aspect of your relationship.

Lesson 2:

Fostering Emotional and Spiritual Intimacy: Emotional and spiritual intimacy deepen the connection in marriage. Investing time and effort in cultivating these aspects of the relationship enhances love, understanding, and unity.

Reflect on a recent meaningful conversation you had with your partner that deepened your emotional or spiritual intimacy. Write a journal entry describing the topics discussed, the emotions felt, and the insights gained. Reflect on the significance of such conversations in your relationship and the impact they have on your bond.

Write a letter to your partner, expressing your desire to foster emotional and spiritual intimacy in your marriage. Share specific ideas or activities that you believe can contribute to this goal, such as setting aside dedicated time for deep conversations, engaging in shared spiritual practices, or expressing gratitude and vulnerability. Discuss how these practices can strengthen your love, understanding, and unity.

_____

_____

_____

_____

_____

_____

_____

_____

_____

_____

_____

_____

_____

_____

_____

_____

_____

_____

_____

_____

_____

_____

_____

_____

_____

_____

_____

Create a list of questions that promote emotional and spiritual intimacy. These questions can be thought-provoking and encourage deeper conversations between you and your partner. Set aside time regularly to ask and answer these questions, allowing yourselves to be vulnerable and create space for growth and connection.

Lesson 3:

Growing Together: Marriage offers opportunities for personal and mutual growth. Couples are called to support each other's aspirations, challenge one another to become the best versions of themselves, and continuously learn and adapt together.

Reflect on a recent instance where your partner supported you in pursuing a personal aspiration or goal. Write a journal entry describing the impact of their support on your growth and the development of your relationship. Reflect on how you can reciprocate this support and create an environment that encourages personal and mutual growth.

Write a letter to your partner, expressing your commitment to supporting each other's aspirations and growth. Share specific ways in which you can actively support their goals and encourage their personal development. Discuss how you can provide a safe and nurturing environment for each other's growth.

Create a vision board or collage together that represents your shared aspirations and goals. Include images, quotes, and symbols that reflect your individual and mutual growth objectives. Display this visual representation in a prominent place as a reminder of your commitment to continuously learn, adapt, and support each other's growth.

Made in the USA
Columbia, SC
28 January 2025